D0206009

Moo-Moo Went the Tuba

By Teresa Domnauer

School Specialty
Publishing

Library of Congress Cataloging-in-Publication Data is on file with the publisher.

Send all inquiries to:
School Specialty Publishing
8720 Orion Place
Columbus, OH 43240-2111

ISBN 0-7696-4232-2

1 2 3 4 5 6 7 8 9 10 PHXBK 10 09 08 07 06 05

Hi, I'm Farkle McBride.
Join me in learning about
the fun sounds that instruments make.
Close your eyes and listen. What do you hear?
Birds sing in the trees. The refrigerator hums.
The school bell rings.
You hear music all around you!

Table of Contents

Thunder 4–5

Rain 6–7

Duck 8–9

Bird 10–11

Horse 12–13

Cow 14–15

Elephant 16–17

Bumblebee 18–19

Rooster 20–21

Rattlesnake 22–23

Doorbell 24–25

Train Whistle 26–27

Heartbeat 28–29

Thinking About It 31–32

Thunder

Close your eyes and listen.
What do you **hear**?
It sounds like
a thunderstorm booming.
But it is the rumble of the kettledrum!
Bang on the kettledrum.
You will hear the sound of thunder.

6

Rain

Close your eyes and listen.
What do you hear?
It sounds like raindrops falling.
But it is a rain stick filled with pebbles!
Turn the rain stick upside down.
You will hear the sound of rain.

Duck

Close your eyes and listen.
What do you hear?
It sounds like a duck quacking.
But it is an oboe's low wail!
Blow into the oboe's **reeds**.
You will hear the sound of a duck.

Bird

Close your eyes and listen.
What do you hear?
It sounds like a bird
singing in a tree.
But it is the sweet music of the flute!
Blow into the flute.
You will hear the sound of a bird.

Horse

Close your eyes and listen.
What do you hear?
It sounds like a horse
clip-clopping.
But it is the knocking of woodblocks!
Tap the woodblocks.
You will hear the sound
of a horse's hooves.

Cow

Close your eyes and listen.
What do you hear?
It sounds like a cow saying "Moo."
But it is the low **tone** of the tuba!
Blow into the tuba.
You will hear the sound of a cow.

Elephant

Close your eyes and listen.
What do you hear?
It sounds like
an elephant's **blaring** call.
But it is the toot of the trumpet!
Blow into the trumpet.
You will hear the sound
of an elephant.

Bumblebee

Close your eyes and listen.
What do you hear?
It sounds like
a bumblebee buzzing.
But it is the **hum** of the bassoon!
Blow into the bassoon.
You will hear the sound
of a bumblebee.

Rooster

Close your eyes and listen.
What do you hear?
It sounds like a rooster crowing.
But it is the blast of the bugle!
Blow into the bugle.
You will hear the sound of a rooster.

Rattlesnake

Close your eyes and listen.
What do you hear?
It sounds like a rattlesnake's tail.
But it is the rattle of the maracas!
Shake the maracas.
You will hear the sound
of a rattlesnake.

Doorbell

Close your eyes and listen.
What do you hear?
It sounds like the doorbell
is ringing.
But it is the **chime** of the xylophone!
Strike the xylophone.
You will hear the sound of a doorbell.

Train Whistle

Close your eyes and listen.
What do you hear?
It sounds like a train's
loud **whistle**.
But it is the harmonica's **shrill tune**!
Blow into the harmonica.
You will hear the sound
of a train whistle.

Heartbeat

Close your eyes and listen.
What do you hear?
It sounds like a heartbeat.
But it is the steady **beat** of the drum!
Bang on the drum.
You will hear the sound
of your heartbeat.

Vocabulary

beat–a musical rhythm. *The beat of the music was fast.*

blaring–having a loud, harsh sound. *The loud blaring trumpet hurt my ears.*

chime–a gentle bell sound. *Our doorbell's chime makes a pleasant sound.*

hear–to take in sound through the ears. *I hear Mom calling my name.*

hum–a low, buzzing sound. *The computer makes a quiet hum when it is turned on.*

reed–a small, specially-shaped piece of wood that attaches to the mouthpiece of woodwind instruments. *Andy blew air over his oboe's reeds.*

shrill–a high, sharp sound. *The police siren made a shrill sound.*

strike–to hit. *Strike the drum with the drumsticks.*

tone–a single sound having strength, length, and pitch. *The tone of the tuba was low and long.*

tune–a string of musical notes that makes a pleasing sound. *I sing a tune while I am working.*

whistle–a sharp, high-pitched sound. *The kettle of boiling water let out a loud whistle.*

Think About It!

1. What instrument does a bumblebee sound like?

2. How would you describe the sound of a xylophone?

3. What animal do the woodblocks sound like?

4. How do you think a bugle and a rooster are alike?

5. What instrument sounds like a songbird?

The Story and You!

1. Close your eyes. What sounds do you hear around you?

2. How could you make music without using a musical instrument?

3. Put your hand over your heart. What sound or instrument does it remind you of?

4. What kind of music do you like to listen to?

5. Do you play a musical instrument? What do you think it sounds like?